In Grief's Lone Hour

John M. Drescher

HERALD PRESS
Scottdale, Pennsylvania
Kitchener, Ontario

The Visitation Pamphlets are directed to specific personal needs. They are designed to be given by pastors, chaplains, doctors, nurses, and all who would share at an appropriate moment words of hope and faith.

Blessings by Your Bedside by John M. Drescher
By Still Waters by John M. Drescher
Empty Arms by Mary Joyce Rae
Facing Illness With Faith by John M. Drescher
For the Golden Years by John M. Drescher
For Hospital Days by Robert W. Rae
Grief's Slow Work by Harold Bauman
I Lift My Eyes by John M. Drescher
In Grief's Lone Hour by John M. Drescher
Just in for Tests by Robert W. Rae
May Your Marriage Be a Happy One by John M. Drescher
Personal Prescriptions by John M. Drescher
Shut In But Not Shut Out by Mary Joyce Rae and Robert W. Rae
Sources of Spiritual Strength by John M. Drescher
Spiritual Nutrients by John M. Drescher
Strength for Suffering by John M. Drescher
Suffering and God's Presence by John M. Drescher
To the New Mother by Helen Good Brenneman
What Can I Say? by Robert W. Rae
Why Suffering? by Paul W. Nisly

IN GRIEF'S LONE HOUR
Copyright © 1971, 1986 by Herald Press, Scottdale, Pa. 15683
    Published simultaneously in Canada by Herald Press,
    Kitchener, Ont. N2G 4M5. All rights reserved.
International Standard Book Number: 0-8361-3425-7
Printed in the United States of America
Cover photo by Anchor/Wallace

91 90 89 88 87 86 15 14 13 12 11 10 9 8 7

Preface

The most shattering experience any of us ever faces is the death of a loved one. It is as though an only light goes out, and we are left to wander in the darkness alone. The loss seems so final; the burden is almost too much to bear. No one has ever found a way to remove the immediate pain of a parting through death. To understand what happens in the experience of grief can help to fortify us in grief's lone hour. But because we love we also grieve. Grief is the natural process that follows an experience of loss. Grief can be healthy. We should look at what happens to us in a grief experience. Simply knowing how our bodies and minds respond to grief helps us to face this experience.

In the message of the gospel we have also a message of hope, love, and life hereafter. We know the end of life here is not ultimate death but life eternal. Just as Christ died and rose from the dead to live forever, so we, who have faith in him, die to live eternally.

This booklet is written to share insights on normal responses to grief and to help point the way to hope. May it help many in grief's lone hour.

The Face of Grief—Death

"What man can live and not see death, or save himself from the power of the grave?" *Psalm 89:48.*

A few years ago some English archaeologists exploring a cave near the site of an ancient Egyptian community came upon a carved coffin. In it were the mummified remains of a little girl. When the inscription was deciphered it read: "O my life, my love, my little one! Would God I had died for you!"

The writer of an account of this discovery tells how these explorers "uncovered their heads and from the darkness of the cave went back with dim eyes into the blazing sunshine of the Egyptian desert." This discovery reminded them again of one of the oldest of all human experiences—death and grief.

"We become shockingly aware that death is a normal part of every life. No life is exempt. Death is the most important thing to prepare for, discuss, and understand. Actually, life is not lived to the fullest when we think of having it stretch on forever. . . . It is thrilling to know that I am in God's powerful hands and sorrow cannot separate me from his love and goodness. What connections!"

The above words from a young mother who lost both her husband and a promising, cheery, blue-eyed child startle us to an awareness—an awareness of death as a part of life. Death is a subject which we do not want to discuss. Yet it is death which all of us shall face sooner or later.

Death is a reality for us. We must face it or we do not face life itself. No one can avoid the certainty of death. Everywhere, every day someone longs for the "touch of a vanished hand and the sound of a voice that is still."

An Eastern legend tells of a woman who lost her child. In her grief she went to the prophet and begged him to restore her child to her. The old man looked long and understandingly at her and then tenderly counseled, "Go and bring me a handful of rice from

4

some house where sorrow has not entered and I shall grant your wish."

Here and there she went but everywhere the reply was the same. In every home was an empty chair. Slowly the sorrows of others touched her own sorrowing heart. Soon her sympathy went out to others. Not only did her own sorrow subside but she found again purpose for living.

Death is the most certain of all certainties. This fact must be faced with candor and faith. The ultimate hope of the Christian lies beyond death and the grave. Christians rest in the promises of God for eternal life. We do not look at death as the grim reaper, hooded and hostile, stalking us all with a scythe. Rather, death is the invitation to the fuller life. We cross the mysterious river to the other side with our hand in the hand of the one who said, "Because I live, you shall live also."

So we are called in death to think not so much on the lifeless body but on the liberated spirit. We believe as the Scripture says, "To die is gain." The Bible insists that "no eye has seen, no ear has heard, no mind has conceived what God has prepared for those who love him" (1 Corinthians 2:9).

Such hope does not remove the sorrow from the heart but it does remove the sense of dread and fear. It means that we do not sorrow as those who have no hope. As Scott says, "Is death the last sleep? No, it is the last final awakening."

Prayer
   O God, Creator of us all, since the beginning of time, generation after generation has gone through the experience of death. Yet to each of us the encounter with death is new. Thank you for the deep assurance that as we have trusted you for our salvation in life, we can know that to die is to be in your presence. Amen.

The Face of Grief—Shock

"Wait for the Lord; be strong and take heart and wait for the Lord."
Psalm 27:14.

Even though all of us know we will face the death of a loved one sooner or later, yet we are in many ways unprepared for this experience. Grief is the natural response to an experience of loss. Shock is the first element of such grief. After death of a loved one the survivor in a sense "passes out" until more ready to face the fact that the loved one is dead.

Shock is God's way of preventing us from breaking completely. It is nature's way of protecting us from unbearable pain and from thinking too much about the future. It can be confused with Christian faith or personal endurance when a person is said to be "taking it well."

Accept the fact that you are in a state of shock. You are dazed from "the blow." None of your reactions is likely to be normal. In a sense this numbness is a blessing because the pain is deadened.

Many at this stage feel like revolting against God. Questions like, How can God do this to me? and Why did God let it happen? are normal. When death takes a loved one, a deep sense of God's presence seems numbed. It may seem that no one, even God, knows, understands, or cares about the grief, sorrow, and heartache you feel.

Try to find a friend, one person, in whom you can confide your inmost feelings and thoughts. Find one who will not sit in judgment, someone who will listen with understanding sympathy, who will understand that grief feelings are right and good. True love cannot accept death quickly. No doubt such a person will be someone who has passed through the same experience.

Do not fear for your sanity if you cannot think clearly or reason rationally. It is not insanity. It is shock you are experiencing.

Other symptoms may normally accompany great grief. Loss

6

of appetite, headache, fitful sleep, tormenting chest pain, and weakness are common. You may decide that you do not know how to think, how to stop feeling, how to start feeling, where to go, where not to go, what to do, what not to do.

Life is like a nightmare, unreal. You may shift between unbelief that your loved one has died and the question, Why did it happen? You may find yourself saying, "I just can't understand it." Helplessness, hopelessness, and loneliness take over. You feel everything has stopped for you and you are startled to see that life for others is going on in a normal way. The sun is still shining and traffic is on the street. You may feel no one else has suffered as you suffer.

In all this certain things must be kept in mind. First, such reactions are a normal part of grief. You must be kind to yourself and forgive yourself for those negative emotions of guilt, self-pity, and bitterness. Express your suffering. Every emotion expressed, whether love, anger, or grief, is a release of pressure.

Place your trust confidently in God's providence. Accidents, calamities, errors of judgment are out of your control and you have a duty to live in the present.

Realize what the psalmist did when he said that God knows his trouble in spite of the darkness of the hour. "I will be glad and rejoice in your love, for you saw my affliction and knew the anguish of my soul" (Psalm 31:7).

Prayer
> Lord God, in the shock of the moment, I do not understand, I do not know, I cannot comprehend what has happened. Help me to really believe that you know and that you are able to sustain me now and always. Amen.

The Face of Grief—Struggle

"Now I know in part; then I shall know fully, even as I am fully known."
1 Corinthians 13:12.

Death comes with finality, but the motion of your life together carries you forward on its momentum as if your loved one still lived. For some time it is difficult to really believe your loved one is gone. You expect to hear the same voice. You expect your loved one to return at regular times. You awake expecting to find your loved one near you.

You may also experience guilt feelings. You have a sense of being responsible in some way for the other's death. You may think, "If only I had taken the first signs of sickness more seriously" or "If only I'd have gone to a different hospital or called the doctor earlier, or had not let them operate." You blame yourself for the unchangeable. Perhaps it is not so much a feeling of guilt as of desperation.

"So spoke Martha also in John 11, 'If you had been here!' But Jesus had been there all the time. He had been with them in deepest sympathy, in kindly thought, in gracious intention, in tender and yet ample plan. What they viewed as a lamentable mischance was a vital part of a larger scheme, begotten and inspired by unfailing love. There was no need for regret; everything was just exactly right.

"And so it is with most of the if's, the remorseful if's that ravage and devastate our peace. They destroy filial trust; they destroy spiritual peace; they destroy the wide sweeping light of Christian hope."—J. H. Jowett.

Anger, hostility, and resentment may take over in times of grief. In deep despair you may blame those nearest and dearest to you—God, the doctor, or other faithful helpers who cared for your loved one before death. You feel betrayed, trapped, frightened.

8

These feelings are normal. They need to be admitted and confessed. You need to ask for strength to rise above them.

If you have made mistakes or if others have, recall that the essence of the gospel is forgiveness. God freely forgives. You are to forgive yourself and others. Otherwise, grief works harm rather than help.

There is no satisfying answer to the question of why the innocent suffer. It will always in this life remain a mystery.

Paul Gerhardt, seventeenth-century pastor who experienced great grief when four of his five children died while very young, tells the secret of victory.

> Commit thou all thy griefs
> And ways into his hands,
> To his sure truth and tender care,
> Who heaven and earth commands.
>
> No profit canst thou gain
> By self-consuming care;
> To him commend thy cause; his ear
> Attends the softest prayer.

Prayer

O God, in my deep sorrow I long to experience that you are able to do above all I ask or think. I bring to you my broken and bereaved heart and pray that you will heal it in your love. I know only in part and look forward to the day when I shall fully know. Amen.

The Face of Grief—Suffering

"For I am convinced that neither death nor life, neither angels nor demons, neither the present nor the future, nor any powers, neither height nor depth, nor anything else in all creation, will be able to separate us from the love of God that is in Christ Jesus our Lord." Romans 8:38-39.

In the next step of grief we begin to accept more fully the fact that death has taken a loved one. We acknowledge this fact and recognize that we are grieving. We now have an uncontrollable urge to express our grief. Our loved one has departed. It is only natural that we feel an aching void. Grief weighs us down and tears flow. The release of emotions is cleansing to our mind and spirit.

A friend of mine, who in a short time lost three family members, wrote, "In addition to finding answers to some questions I received several insights about grief. If persons cry at a funeral, people say they are taking it hard. If they do not cry people say they are standing up well. What is normal? What is Christian?

"One hard lesson I had to learn was that it is not a sign of weak faith to cry. I was amazed to read in Acts 8:2 that 'godly men buried Stephen, and mourned deeply for him.' Also Acts 20:37 and 38 tells us that as Paul was leaving Ephesus for Jerusalem, the elders 'all wept as they embraced [Paul] and kissed him. What grieved them most was his statement that they would never see his face again.'

"Weeping is simply God's method for us to release emotion. A strong physical body or a strong faith in God does not keep a Christian from having emotion when death comes close. It is appropriate and Christian to release our emotions in the way God intended. To suppress deep emotions may lead to a serious emotional upheaval some weeks or months following the funeral. Such persons are like a teakettle with no opening for the steam to escape. Eventually there is an explosion."

This friend further testifies, "Another lesson I learned was that it is not necessarily a sign of selfishness or self-pity to sorrow over the loss of a close friend. How often you hear a bereaved person say, 'I really shouldn't be so sad because of this loss. It is selfishness that makes me wish the person were still here, but somehow it feels like a part of me is gone.'

"True, there may be an element of selfishness, but actually life is made up of relationships with people. Persons with close friends who trust, respect, and accept them are usually happy persons. Persons with no friends are almost dead while they live. Life is made up of friendships. Therefore, when a close friend is taken, a part of you is suddenly gone. It is almost like amputating part of your life or tearing an arm from the body and it takes a long time for the wound to heal and the loss to be replaced.

"The sorrow of the past has been painful, but an honest facing of death has been rewarding. From a physical point of view, death is no longer a cause for dreaded fear. Those who have observed hundreds of deaths report that it usually comes 'peaceful and painless.' They say it is something like going to sleep because death brings its own anesthetic.

"From a spiritual viewpoint, death is the next step in our pilgrimage from earth to heaven. Like Christian in *Pilgrim's Progress*, we hesitate to cross the cold waters of Jordan to reach the Celestial City, but this is a part of God's journey to his city and we need not fear. Of course, we can only have this confidence if we are like Christian."

Prayer:
   O God, my Father, I have learned through giving to keep. I know also that on the occasion of a death of a dear friend, your Son Jesus shared my humanity and wept. Thank you that sorrow endures only for the night and joy comes in the morning and that nothing can separate me from your love. Amen.

The Face of Grief—Strength

"When you pass through the waters, I will be with you; and when you pass through the rivers, they will not sweep over you." *Isaiah 43:2.*

"My presence will go with you, and I will give you rest." *Exodus 33:14.*

In his address *Courage,* Sir James Barrie quotes one who says that God gives us memory so that we may have roses in December. Memory is good. It helps us recall the past and our beloved. But when memory makes us unable to return to the normal and usual activities, if it turns into something which holds us back, we use memory wrongly. God wants us also to look forward. A grieving heart looks back with anguish. A surrendered heart looks forward in confidence.

It is natural to remember, to recall, what life with our loved one meant. But how do we handle memory? We were enriched together. But it is just as important to remind ourselves that nothing we can do or say, no labor or sacrifice can bring our loved one back. We suffer, not because we do not know death will someday come, but because we are not prepared for separation.

That separation is so real we may many times regress into suffering long after the death of our loved one. Birthdays, anniversaries, holidays, and meeting of old friends are particularly difficult times. The pain of grief strikes at such times because we remember many things.

We are compelled to make adjustments, although it is difficult to do so. Now is the time to force ourselves to begin to discover who we are, what we want, where we belong, and what we want to do. It is dangerous during these early days to make major and irreversible decisions. Sometimes people make vows to God in haste or they sell their home, move away, or change jobs, which may not in time prove wise. We should be slow to make major changes in times of grief.

Time is one of God's gracious provisions for us. A young

father whose son had died suddenly said to me, "I've learned that time is a great healer." So it is. Yes, the healing process is slow. There will continue to be empty days with almost unbearable loneliness and pain. Grief will be so deep at times it will cause a disinterest in life itself. But it is also true as God promises, "Your strength will equal your days" (Deuteronomy 33:25).

So the deep wound of sorrow, gradually healed by the sunlight of God's love, the friendships of others, and the challenge of daily duties grows less painful. Always something of the scar remains but it is healed and the pain is gone.

> Time like an ever-rolling stream
> Bears all our griefs away.

Sorrow, perhaps more than anything else, can throw us into the merciful arms of God. He does not desire our heartbreak but he uses it to draw us to himself. He promises not only to be with us in the waters of sorrow but also in the days ahead as we make our memories milestones rather than millstones. For we find that even our experience of grief can give us added strength as we realize more fully than ever before our need for complete dependence each day upon God.

Prayer
O God, thank you for precious memories of my loved one. They help sustain me in this hour of grief. Don't let the memories make me live in the past. Rather, make even this separation from one loved by you and me the means of growing confidence in your care and growing usefulness in your kingdom. Amen.

The Face of Grief—Recovery

"For you, O Lord, have delivered my soul from death, my eyes from tears, my feet from stumbling, that I may walk before the Lord in the land of the living." *Psalm 116:8-9.*

The final part of the experience of grief one might call recovery. This speaks of the readjustment to reality. We gradually are aware of the unreality of many of our attitudes and feelings regarding the loved one who has died. We accept our loss. We gain new understanding of death, of God's will, and our purpose for living.

This readjustment to reality is not a return to our "old self" but a movement to a "better self" because from grief we experience a stronger self. When we realize we can never return to where we were, we are well on the way to recovery from grief. We see death in a new way—not an extinction, an end, a dreaded door to oblivion but as the gate to life everlasting. We see that at death we bury only the body of our loved one. The soul moves on. The painful burden of sorrow dissolves slowly and out of the bleak suffering emerges a new strength and wisdom.

Now we understand the eternal more clearly. After the resurrection the apostles never used the word death to express the close of a Christian's earthly life. They referred to a Christian who has passed on as "at home with the Lord," and used phrases such as "to depart and be with Christ" and "to sleep in Jesus."

F. B. Meyer a few days before his death wrote to a friend, "I have just heard, to my surprise, that I have only a few more days to live. It may be that, before this reaches you, I shall have entered the Palace. Don't trouble to answer. We shall meet in the morning."

When the great Puritan, Owen, lay on his deathbed his secretary wrote (in his name) to a friend, "I am still in the land of the living." "Stop," said Owen. "Change that and say, I am yet in

14

the land of the dying, but I hope soon to be in the land of the living."

There is no death! The stars go down
To rise upon some other shore,
And bright in heaven's jeweled crown
They shine for evermore.
—John Luckey McCreery

Recovery means to return to normal living. Some find this not only difficult to do but feel that by so doing they express lack of affection for the departed loved one. Surely the person who passed on would want us to carry on nobly, to live life to the full. We must fight the morbid feeling to cling to the past.

Grief can give us a new vision of what our task is. As one writer put it, "At long last, almost all grievers believe they are alive for a specific purpose. There is a purpose for this life." For the Christian it is to fulfill the will of God.

Clement H. Pugsley gives a helpful formula in facing grief. He tells us to "commit our grief to God and avoid the two dangers of self-sufficiency and self-pity." Resolve not to live in the past but to face the future with hope and courage. Decide not to spend the days dreaming about the future. Hear God's call now in the present circumstances. Recognize the need for constant prayer, for ourselves and others. Respond to the need for fellowship, especially the fellowship of the church. Resolve to cultivate a thankful and adoring heart.

George Matheson, a blind poet who knew much grief, expressed it this way (let it be our prayer):

O love that will not let me go,
I rest my weary soul in thee;
I give thee back the life I owe,
That in thine ocean depths its flow
May richer, fuller be.

For Divine Strength

Father, in thy mysterious presence kneeling,
Fain would our souls feel all thy kindling love;
For we are weak, and need some deep revealing
Of trust and strength and calmness from above.

Lord, we have wandered forth through doubt and sorrow,
And thou hast made each step an onward one;
And we will ever trust each unknown morrow,
Thou wilt sustain us till its work is done.

In the heart's depths a peace serene and holy
Abides; and when pain seems to have its will,
Or we despair, O may that peace rise slowly,
Stronger than agony, and we be still!

Now, Father, now, in thy dear presence kneeling,
Our spirits yearn to feel thy kindling love:
Now make us strong—we need thy deep revealing
Of trust and strength and calmness from above.
—Samuel Johnson.

1 Corinthians 15:51-58

Listen, I tell you a mystery:
We will not all sleep, but we will all be changed—in a flash, in the twinkling of an eye, at the last trumpet.
For the trumpet will sound, the dead will be raised imperishable, and we will be changed.
For the perishable must clothe itself with the imperishable, and the mortal with immortality.
When the perishable has been clothed with the imperishable, and the mortal with immortality, then the saying that is written will come true: "Death has been swallowed up in victory."

Where, O death, is your victory?
Where, O death, is your sting?

The sting of death is sin, and the power of sin is the law. But thanks be to God! He gives us the victory through our Lord Jesus Christ.
Therefore ... stand firm. Let nothing move you. Always give yourselves fully to the work of the Lord, because you know that your labor in the Lord is not in vain.